Jane Ery

Holst

Other books in this series

The Great Composers

Holst

Imogen Holst

FABER & FABER   LONDON AND BOSTON

First published in 1974
by Faber and Faber Limited
3 Queen Square London WC1N 3AU
Second edition 1981
Filmset and printed in Great Britain by
BAS Printers Limited
Over Wallop Hampshire

British Library Cataloguing in Publication Data

Holst, Imogen
   Holst.—2nd ed.—(The Great composers)
   1. Holst, Gustav
   I. Title   II. Series
   780'.92'4   ML410.H7
   ISBN 0-571-18032-9

Contents

Illustrations

Music Examples

(The facsimile manuscript music extracts are listed under *Illustrations.*)

9

Acknowledgements

I wish to express my thanks to the following, who have kindly allowed me to reproduce copyright material: to Boosey and Hawkes Music Publishers Ltd for the music example on page 36; to Novello and Co. Ltd (pages 36–7, 58, 62–3); to Stainer and Bell Ltd (pages 38–9, 45); to the Oxford University Press for the plainsong on page 39 and the music example on page 66; to J. & W. Chester Ltd (page 44); to Faber Music Ltd for the music example on pages 79–81 and (for J. Curwen and Sons Ltd) the examples on pages 67 and 85; to R. Smith and Co. Ltd (pages 68–9); to John Gay for the photograph of Holst in 1933 by Martha Stern on the front cover; to the Holst Birthplace Museum Trust, Cheltenham for the photograph on page 14; to the William Morris Gallery, Walthamstow for the photograph on page 22; to Ursula Vaughan Williams for the drawing on page 23; to the National Portrait Gallery, London for the portrait on page 33; to Alexander Walker for the illustrations on pages 41, 47, 61; to John Agate for the photograph on page 43; to Edward Pollitzer for the photograph on page 56; to Sydney J. Loeb for the photograph on page 65; to the Administrator of the Thomas Hardy Estate for permission to reproduce the letter on page 71; to the Executors of the Britten Estate for the facsimile on page 73; to the Trustees of the British Library for the facsimile on page 75; to Elliott and Fry for the photograph on page 77; and to the Syndics of the Fitzwilliam Museum, Cambridge for permission to reproduce the manuscript of the first movement of the *Brook Green Suite* on the back cover. (The reproductions on pages 25 and 31 are non-copyright. All other illustrations are copyright G. & I. Holst Ltd.)
    I am also grateful to Ursula Vaughan Williams and the Oxford University Press for quotations from *Heirs and Rebels* and *R. V. W.—A Biography of Ralph Vaughan Williams*; to the Trustees of the Hardy Estate, and Macmillan, London and Basingstoke, the Macmillan Company of Canada and the Macmillan Company of New York for

quotations from Hardy's *The Return of the Native*; to Macmillan, London and Basingstoke, for quotations from Stanford's *Musical Composition*; to the Clarendon Press, Oxford, for lines from Bridges' *Ode to Music*; to Thames and Hudson (American edition, McGraw-Hill Book Co.) for quotations from Philip Henderson's *William Morris*; to A. R. Mowbray and Co. Ltd and Elizabeth Twistington Higgins for the description of Holst on page 30 from her *Still Life*; to the unknown copyright owner of William Vowles's article *Gustav Holst with the Army*, published in the *Musical Times*, September 1934; to the Morley College Magazine for the quotation on page 42; to the Librarian of the University of Glasgow for his courtesy in making available to me copies of the text of Holst's letters to W. G. Whittaker, and to the Honorary Curator of the Holst Birthplace Museum in Cheltenham for providing me with information about my father's ancestors.

I am particularly grateful to the Oxford University Press for giving me permission to quote letters and other documentary information already published in my book *Gustav Holst: a Biography* (Oxford, 2nd edition 1969), and to Faber Music Ltd and G. & I. Holst Ltd. for allowing me to quote from several of my Commentaries in the 1974 *A Thematic Catalogue of Gustav Holst's Music*.

11

I *A native of Cheltenham*

Gustav Holst was born in a small house in Cheltenham, Gloucestershire, on 21st September 1874. He was christened Gustavus Theodore
von Holst after his grandfather Gustavus, a composer of elegant pieces
for the harp, and his great-uncle Theodor, a painter of romantic
pictures. His grandfather, who had been born in Riga, Latvia, was the
first of the von Holsts to have married an Englishwoman and to have
earned his living in England. He established himself in the fashionable
town of Cheltenham during the eighteen-forties, giving lessons to all
the young ladies whose mothers wished them to learn the harp or the
piano. His son Adolph continued the family tradition of teaching the
piano—a tradition that had already begun in the eighteenth century
with great-grandfather Matthias of Riga. Adolph also gave frequent
recitals at the Assembly Rooms and played the organ every Sunday in
the newly-built Gothic church of All Saints. The proceeds from the
recitals only just covered his expenses, but his salary as organist and
choirmaster enabled him to marry one of his pupils. She was a Miss
Clara Lediard of Cirencester, whose singing was much admired in the
neighbourhood: it was said that'she threw an abundance of feeling into
all she attempted'.

Gustav was their first child. His earliest recollections were of hearing
his father playing Mendelssohn. Adolph was a real pianist, with a clear,
singing touch and an insatiable passion for hard work. He once told a
friend: 'I have been practising a passage in octaves for at least five years
off and on, and it isn't right yet, so I have never played the piece in
public.' At All Saints church the singers spoke of him as 'a stern
exacting choirmaster', and he was known to have said to a struggling
pupil: 'If you are not clever at present, make yourself so.' Cheltenham
audiences appreciated his 'Musical Afternoons', loudly applauding 'the
excellent performances of high-class classical music of varied and   13

The house in Cheltenham where Holst was born

instructive character'. But his own family found him an uncomfortable person to live with. He used to spend his free evenings practising the piano in a warehouse at the back of the local music shop, and he once admitted that his ideal of domestic happiness was to live on the top floor of a well-run hotel.

Gustav's mother died when he was only eight years old. He was a delicate child, suffering from asthma and troubled by weak eyesight: he could never manage to keep pace with his robust young brother Emil. He was looked after by his aunt Nina von Holst, a pianist who had once strewn rose-petals for Liszt to walk on. A few years later, his father

Holst at the age of eleven

married another pupil. She was a theosophist, and she got into the habit of inviting other theosophists to the house for meetings. Gustav used to listen to their earnest talks about reincarnation, and would then describe them, the next day, to his friends at the Cheltenham Grammar School.

He began composing when he was about twelve, having been inspired by the poem 'Horatius' which he had been given to learn for home-work. Many years later, when a friend asked him about this early effort, he said: 'It was the result of knowing Berlioz's book on "Instrumentation" not wisely but too well, and of not knowing anything else about the

15

theory of music. I wrote it at odd moments in my bedroom. Previous to that I had had it ringing in my head when walking. (I was a good walker, and an incessant one.)' The manuscript full score of *Horatius* stops abruptly on page 20 in the middle of a bar. He had had to wait until his father was out of the house before trying it over on the piano, and when he heard what it sounded like he was so shocked that he never added another note.

During his last two years at school his attempts at composition were not so ill-fated. There were piano pieces; organ voluntaries; settings of poems by Scott, Hood, Campbell and Kingsley; anthems, including a vesper hymn with a verse for 'hidden chorus'; and, in 1892, a *Symphony in C minor,* 'begun Jan. 11th, finished Feb. 5th'. These dates, so triumphantly inserted on the title-page of the score, are misleading. They suggest that he wrote quickly and fluently, but he was a slow worker, and during these years he was groping insecurely, with little to guide him. His father gave him no help with composition, preferring to concentrate on training him to become a concert pianist.

When Gustav was seventeen he was appointed organist and choirmaster of Wyck Rissington, a village in the Cotswold hills, at a salary of £4 a year. This was his first professional engagement, and it taught him a good deal about teaching. He soon made friends with his choir-boys, and forty years later he was still corresponding with his first harmonium pupil. A few miles from Wyck Rissington, at the village of Bourton-on-the-Water, he was invited to conduct the Choral Society in John Farmer's oratorio *Christ and His Soldiers,* with a choir and orchestra of fifty performers. He knew nothing about conducting, but he plunged straight into his first rehearsal, learning by trial and error. One of his friends has mentioned that 'when he heard of a lady harpist who was staying in the neighbourhood, he persuaded her to play in the work prepared by the Choral Society. Of course, there was no harp part; but he, by playing to her on the piano, showed her the sort of music he wanted, and she, by playing to him on the harp, showed him how it would sound best on her instrument.' Apparently the result of the part that he wrote for her made a deep impression on the audience.

Walking from one choir practice to another, he learnt to know this stretch of the Cotswold hills by heart, and he never forgot the steep, narrow lanes, or the distant view across each valley, or the mellow grey of the stone walls and cottages and farms. It was always to remain his favourite part of England.

16

In his last year at home before going to college, someone—perhaps his stepmother—suggested that he should consult a phrenologist who was then in Cheltenham. Phrenology, 'the study of the structure of the bones enclosing the brain as an indication of the various faculties', was still highly thought of, and an 'analysis' was listened to with respect. On this occasion, Gustav was told: 'You possess a large brain, but unfortunately the vitality is not equal to the brain power. You are by nature active. You will not be very fluent as a speaker, but as a writer you will be copious. Upon religious matters you will be decidedly sceptical. You will not mind much where you live, and you can readily make yourself at home in new places. You will be most kind in your manner towards other people. You undervalue your own powers considerably, and you think too little of yourself generally.'

It is true that at this time he had very little confidence. There had been modest successes at the Musical Afternoons when he had played his own piano pieces and had been 'twice encored'. And in February 1893 his comic operetta, *Lansdown Castle, or The Sorcerer of Tewkesbury*, was produced at the Corn Exchange. The Gloucestershire newpapers pointed out that 'like all comic operas of recent date it more or less followed the lines of Gilbert and Sullivan', but they agreed that 'it did great credit to the young composer, and gave promise of future achievements'. This was all very well, but Gustav already knew enough to realize that his efforts were in a different world from the music he had heard at the Three Choirs Festival or on his rare visits to London.

He was grateful when his father allowed him to spend two months in Oxford having lessons in counterpoint. This gave him the encouragement he so much needed, for he found, at last, that there was something that he felt he could do well. After many discussions with the family it was decided that he should go to London to study at the Royal College of Music.

It must have been a relief to get away from home. But he never lost touch with his friends, and throughout his life he used to refer to Cheltenham as his 'native town'.

II *At the Royal College of Music*

When Holst left Cheltenham in May 1893 he was feeling bewildered and depressed. He had failed in his attempt to win an open scholarship for composition at the Royal College of Music, and it was not until two years later that he was to be successful. He was worried because his father was having to pay for his tuition fees at the college. And, as a new student, he was scared of his professors, not knowing what to expect of them.

His first glimpse of the Director, Dr. Hubert Parry, was reassuring, and he was much impressed by one of his lectures on musical history. Many years later he wrote an account of it for his own students who had never known Parry. 'He began in quite an ordinary way,' he told them, 'giving names and dates and events, and I settled down to listen to the sort of lecture I had often heard before. Then he looked up from his notes and said: "I suppose you all know what was going on in Europe at that time?" He then stood up and while walking about he gave us, so it seemed to me, a vision rather than a lecture—a vision of people struggling to express themselves in war, in commerce, in art, in life: a vision of the unity that lay under these various forms of human effort: a vision of the unity of a certain century with those that preceded and followed it: a vision that I learnt from that moment to call History.'

Parry's friendly interest in the students must have been a help to Holst at that time, for he was suffering from neuritis in his right arm and he had been told that he must give up all hope of becoming a pianist. His arm was to trouble him, on and off, for the rest of his life, and there were many occasions when it hurt so much that he could hardly write. The pain was particularly bad during the eighteen-nineties: he was sometimes unable to hold a pen, and he had to tie a nib to his forefinger and draw his hand slowly across the page.

It was essential that he should be able to play an instrument professionally, and he was advised to take up the trombone instead of the piano. This cured his asthma. It also taught him about orchestration from the player's point of view. And it enabled him to earn enough to pay the rent for his bed-sitting-room near Hammersmith Broadway. Even when he had been awarded a scholarship at the college, the maintenance grant was too small to cover his living expenses. By playing the trombone on the pier at seaside resorts every summer and in London theatres throughout the pantomime season he was able to afford the necessities of life: board and lodging, manuscript paper, and tickets for standing room in the gallery at Covent Garden Opera House on Wagner evenings.

Like many other young composers Holst was enthralled by the sound of Wagner's music. Waves of chromatic sequences swept over him, filling his nights and days with unsatisfied cadences, while ill-assimilated wisps of *Tristan* inserted themselves on nearly every page of his own songs and overtures.

His composition teacher, Stanford, greeted his efforts with the comment: 'It won't do, me boy; it won't do.' Part-songs and movements for string sextet were heavily corrected, week after week, with a purple indelible pencil. (Holst afterwards kept these manuscripts on the bottom shelf of a cupboard, in bulky parcels tied up in brown paper and labelled 'Early Horrors'.)

Stanford encouraged his pupils to be practical. He advised them to ask a singer to try through any difficult passages in their songs, so that they would be convinced that it was a mistake to write high notes on awkward syllables. He suggested that they should cue-in alternative instruments in any orchestral piece, so that the music would still make sense even if some of the players were missing. 'Counterpoint teaches economy of material,' he assured his students, and Holst was to prove it, over and over again, in his own music. 'A beginner must not think about originality,' said Stanford: 'if he has it in his nature, it will come out. Let the imagination run, and *criticise it for yourself*, after it has had its fling.'

In his struggles to learn this never-ending lesson of criticizing what he was writing, Holst had the help of his fellow-student Ralph Vaughan Williams. They had become friends at their first meeting in 1895, and they used to play each other their latest compositions while they were still working at them. 'What one really learns from a college', Vaughan Williams wrote long afterwards, 'is not so much from one's official

His 1897 setting of a poem in Phantastes

teachers as from one's fellow-students. We used to meet at a little tea-shop in Kensington and discuss every subject under the sun from the lowest note of the double bassoon to the philosophy of Thomas Hardy's *Jude the Obscure.*' Holst flourished in the warmth of this new companionship. He was no longer bewildered or miserable. He still looked 'too thin and too pale', according to one of his contemporaries, but he was feeling much more confident. In the college archives there is a mention of the meetings of the Literary and Debating Society at which he spoke on 'The Future of English Music', and proposed 'That Academic Training should be Abolished'. (Alas, there is no record of what he said.)

While discussing everything under the sun with his fellow-students he learnt about some of the contemporary poets of the eighteen-nineties, and among his 'Early Horrors' there are settings of poems by George Meredith, Francis Thompson, and the future poet laureate, Robert Bridges, who was afterwards to become his friend. The three writers who influenced him more than anyone else at this time were George Macdonald, Walt Whitman, and William Morris. He was stirred by the romanticism of Macdonald's *Phantastes*: perhaps it reminded him of his great-uncle Theodor's painting of Faust that hung in the music-room at

Cheltenham. The description of the hall in the enchanted castle, 'filled with a subdued crimson light', made a great impression on him, and its 'dull red glow' became an indispensable stage direction in each of his early unperformed operas. Twentieth-century readers of *Phantastes* may find it embarrassing to have to pick their way past all those fairies and snowdrops and butterflies: it is difficult not to lose patience with Macdonald's preference for a ghostly wife who would disappear at dusk and for a phantom baby that would wait about in a forest until it was fetched. But Holst found other things in the book, beyond the romantic apparitions. He found the question: 'How can beauty and ugliness dwell so near?' And he found the statement: 'What we call evil is the only and best shape, which, for the person and his condition at the time, could be assumed by the best good.'

In Whitman's poems he found robust acknowledgement of his 'vision of unity':

> *O I know that those men and women were not for nothing*
> *any more than we are for nothing,*
> *I know that they belong to the scheme of the world every bit*
> *as much as we now belong to it.*

This 'modern' freedom of rhythm was so exciting that it suggested music to him:

> *O to realize space!*
> *The plenteousness of all, that there are no bounds,*
> *To emerge and be of the sky, of the sun and moon and flying*
> *clouds, as one with them.*

He wanted to set some of the verses, but his technique was not yet equal to the challenge, and he strained himself in the attempt. It was not until many years later that he was able to pay his debt of gratitude to Whitman in the music of *A Dirge for Two Veterans* and his *Ode to Death*.

From William Morris he learnt about socialism. 'I do not want art for a few', Morris had written, 'any more than education for a few, or freedom for a few. I want all persons to be educated according to their capacity, not according to the amount of money which their parents happen to have. I want those who do the rough work of the world, sailors, miners, and the like, to be paid abundant money-wages, and to have plenty of leisure.'

William Morris's house in Hammersmith

Morris was still living in Kelmscott House, Hammersmith, at the time when Holst was a student. This beautiful house overlooking the river Thames was the headquarters of the Hammersmith Socialist Society. Holst became a member, and listened to lectures on Sunday evenings by Bernard Shaw and other socialists, including the sixty-year-old Morris, who then had only two more years to live. Holst set several of Morris's poems which he had discovered in the hand-printed editions of the Kelmscott Press. One of the workers in the Press was an amateur musician who made friends with him: he gave him a proof page of the famous Kelmscott Press edition of Chaucer's *The Canterbury Tales* which Holst kept all his life.

The lectures on socialism were held in a long narrow room which has been described as 'a frugal meeting-place with bare floor and matting on the white-washed walls; there were wooden chairs and forms, and a

22

plain kitchen table on the platform'. It was here that Holst was invited to be the first conductor of the Hammersmith Socialist Choir. A programme that has survived since 1897 shows that he taught them madrigals by Morley, dramatic choruses by Purcell, extracts from two Wagner operas, Mozart's *Ave Verum*, and his own setting of Kingsley's *Song of the River*. One of the sopranos in the choir was a fair-haired, blue-eyed girl called Isobel Harrison. She was the most beautiful person he had ever seen, and although at first she was not much impressed by his appearance, they eventually became engaged, knowing that they would have to wait several years until they could afford to be married.

In 1898 the college authorities offered him an extension of his scholarship for another year, but he decided to refuse it. He had been there long enough. He was grateful for what he had been taught, but the time had come for him to 'learn by doing'. Later on, he wrote to Vaughan Williams, saying: 'When under a master I instinctively try to please him, whereas our business is to learn to please ourselves, which is far more difficult as it is so hard to find out what we want. I believe that really the only good that will last will be done by struggling away on our own.'

III *Translating Sanskrit*

Soon after leaving college he happened to read a book by R. W. Fraser called *Silent Gods and Sun-steeped Lands*. Here he learnt, for the first time, about the ancient Hindu legends of the gods and goddesses of fire, earth, water, sky and storm. He was so excited by what he read that he began to look for other books on Indian literature, and when he came across the collection of sacred verses called 'Rig Veda' he knew that he had found what he wanted for setting to music. But the translations were unsatisfactory: he complained that they were either 'misleading renderings in colloquial English', or else 'strings of English words with no meanings to an English mind'. He searched in the British Museum to see what else was available, but the large volumes that were brought to him were all in the original Sanskrit, and he crept out of the Reading Room feeling more of a fool than he had ever felt before.

He decided that he would have to learn Sanskrit so that he could make his own version of the songs he wanted to set. It was a courageous decision, for he was no good at European languages, and he was already hard at work as a trombone player, touring with orchestras and opera companies in order to save enough money to get married. With characteristic determination he enrolled as a student at the University College, London. His teacher was Dr. Mabel Bode, an Irishwoman with a great sense of humour, who was always known as 'Patsy'. He was her first pupil in Sanskrit. She told him that the gods of the Rig Veda were 'very human people, and human failings were expected of them: Indra, the god of rain, was only really satisfied when his worshippers had made him drunk. The most important gods were Agni, god of fire, who was the friend, brother and guest of men, and Varuna, god of the sky and the waters, who was the friend and judge to whom one came to ask forgiveness—whose boat was called the boat of safety.' After she had taught him the Sanskrit alphabet, and a fair amount of the difficult

॥ संहितापाठः ॥

॥ ॐ ॥

॥ १ ॥ १–९ मधुच्छंदा वैश्वामित्रः ॥ अग्निः ॥ गायत्री ॥

॥ १ ॥ अग्निमीळे पुरोहितं यज्ञस्य देवमृत्विजं । होतारं
रत्नधातमं ॥ १ ॥ अग्निः पूर्वेभिर्ऋषिभिरीड्यो नूतनैरुत । स
देवाँ एह वक्षति ॥ २ ॥ अग्निना रयिमश्नवत्पोषमेव दिवेदिवे ।
यशसं वीरवत्तमं ॥ ३ ॥ अग्ने यं यज्ञमध्वरं विश्वतः परिभूरसि ।
स इद्देवेषु गच्छति ॥ ४ ॥ अग्निर्होता कविक्रतुः सत्यश्चित्रश्रव-
स्तमः । देवो देवेभिरा गमत् ॥ ५ ॥ १ ॥ यदंग दाशुषे त्वमग्ने

Sanskrit text

grammar, he managed during the next few years to translate nearly
thirty hymns and odes which he set for solo voice or for chorus and
orchestra. He was not a poet, and there are occasions when his verses
seem naïve. But they never sound vague or slovenly, for he had set
himself the task of finding words that would be 'clear and dignified', and
that would 'lead the listener into another world'.

He never went to India, and he had no chance of studying Indian
music, but he became so absorbed in the imagined sounds and colours
and rhythms of his chosen 'other world' that he was able to break away
from the conventions of nineteenth-century Europe when he wrote his
short Indian opera *Savitri*. The libretto is his own version of an incident
from the 'Mahabharata', a collection of legends about the descendants
of a great king of ancient India. The story is of Savitri, the wife of a
woodman, who hears the voice of Death calling for her husband
Satyavan. When Death enters, she welcomes him as 'the Just One', and
he is so moved by her greeting that he promises to grant her anything
she asks except the life of her husband. She asks for her own life 'in its
fullness', and when Death agrees triumphantly points out to him that
life in its fullness would be impossible without Satyavan. Death realizes
that he has been defeated and he walks away into the forest. This
startlingly original opera, with its three soloists, small hidden choir,
and orchestra of twelve players, was the first English chamber opera
since the end of the seventeenth century.

There are historians who like to divide up a composer's life into different 'periods': they have labelled Holst's 'Sanskrit period' as beginning in 1899, when he wrote the libretto of his unperformed opera *Sita* (which he afterwards described as 'good old Wagnerian bawling'), and ending in about 1912, when he revised his ode for chorus and orchestra called *The Cloud Messenger*. In real life, however, a composer seldom fits himself into such a neat pattern. It would be a mistake to suppose that Holst lost interest in his Indian studies after 1912, just because *The Cloud Messenger* was the last of his Sanskrit works. To the end of his life he was still influenced by the Hindu philosophy that he had first heard of in 1899. In a letter written to Vaughan Williams, nearly thirty years later, he said: 'I still believe in the Hindu doctrine of Dharma, which is one's path in life. If one is lucky (or maybe unlucky— it doesn't matter) to have a clearly appointed path to which one comes naturally whereas any other one is an unsuccessful effort, one ought to stick to the former. And I am oriental enough to believe in doing so without worrying about the "fruits of action", that is, success or otherwise.'

IV   *The struggle to earn a living*

He married Isobel Harrison in the summer of 1901 and they went to live in two furnished rooms over a shop in Shepherds Bush, near Hammersmith. He was away on tour a good deal of the time, playing trombone in the Carl Rosa Opera Company or in the Scottish Orchestra. When he was able to be in London he had to earn his living by dressing up in a white-and-gold uniform and playing in the White Viennese Band under a conductor called Stanislas Wurm, who was always referred to as 'the Worm': during the interval between their 'selections', members of the band were ordered to speak with a convincing foreign accent if anyone happened to be listening.

His salary as a trombone player was only just enough to live on. He had not been able to afford a honeymoon, but when his father died, he inherited a small legacy and in the spring of 1903, he decided to go to Germany with his wife for a holiday. It was while they were in Berlin, listening to concerts and meeting musicians at the house of his second cousin Matthias, that be began to feel dissatisfied with his previous attempts to be a composer. He wrote to Vaughan Williams, saying:

> I have been trying to think where we (you and I) are and what we ought to do. (Being together so much, I think we work along in much the same way, but I may be wrong.) To begin with, I think we crawl along too slowly—of course it is something to get along at all and I do think our progress is very genuine—but there ought to be more. Somehow we seem too comfortable—we don't seem to strain every nerve. Anyhow, I know I don't. I think we are 'all right' in a mild sort of way. But then mildness is the very devil. So something must happen and we must make it happen. Of course the matter is made rather worse for me owing to lack of cash, and I feel more and more that my mode of living is very unsatisfactory. It was not so bad in

27

*Holst and his wife
in Berlin, 1903*

London when I did a fair amount of writing every day, but the Worm
is a wicked and loathsome waste of time—it makes me so sick of
everything that I cannot settle down to work properly. I think it
would be a great thing for me if I could always live in London and say
goodbye to the Worm and all seaside bands. I should be sorry to leave
the Scottish Orchestra for some things, but it would really be better
on the whole. I will even accept your offer of lending me money rather
than play two or three times a day. I feel it would be so splendid to 'go
into training' as it were, in order to make one's music as beautiful as
possible. And I am sure that after a few months' steady grind we
should have made the beginning of our own 'atmospheres', and so we
should not feel the need of going abroad so much. For it is all that
makes up an 'atmosphere' that we lack in England. Here, people
actually seem anxious to hear new music; still more wonderful, they
even seem anxious to find out all about a new composer! That in itself
would work a revolution in England.

His 'steady grind' in London during the rest of 1903 may eventually have helped to make his music more beautiful, but it had no immediate results in helping him to earn enough to live on. Very few of his works were performed at this time. Two or three of his part-songs had been sung at the St. James's Hall, and there had been a charity concert in Langham Place, 'under the Patronage of the Ladies' Kennel Association', when 'Herr von Holst' had conducted a group of his short pieces for string orchestra. But such opportunities were rare. The Bournemouth Orchestra's performance in 1902 of his *Cotswolds Symphony,*with its slow movement in memory of William Morris, had been a unique occasion of agonized excitement. (In the middle of the only rehearsal, when members of the orchestra were still correcting wrong notes in the parts, several of the woodwind and brass had had to go out and play selections on the pier.)

Publishers were not interested in the *Cotswolds Symphony*, or in any of his other early orchestral works such as the *Walt Whitman Overture* or the *Symphonic Poem: Indra*. The only things that had yet been published were about a dozen short part-songs, and he had had to sell them, one after another, for a sum that barely covered a fortnight's living expenses. In the hope of earning more money he began writing what he called 'pot-boilers'. They were little songs or pieces for violin and piano which were often founded on one or other of the 'Early Horrors', for, as he confessed to Vaughan Williams, he had 'got into the way of thinking that anything would do'. He succeeded in getting several of the pot-boilers published, but as he always had to part with the copyright they brought in very little money.

It is difficult for us to imagine a time when composers had no performing fees or royalties from recordings to live on. At the beginning of this century, no young composer could earn a regular income just by writing music. Holst realized this before very long, and he had almost reached the stage of wondering how to get the next meal when he was rescued by the offer of a teaching appointment at the James Allen's Girls' School at Dulwich, in south-east London. His singing-classes must have seemed astonishingly unconventional. One of his ex-pupils has described an early performance of a part-song he wrote for the school: 'I remember the choir singing and walking off along a corridor and shutting themselves in a far-off room getting softer and softer— leaving the audience straining their ears for the last note.'

Soon afterwards he was appointed Musical Director at St. Paul's   29

Girls' School, Hammersmith: this was his biggest teaching post, and the only one that he kept until the time of his death. An ex-pupil of the school has a vivid recollection of a singing lesson he gave to the juniors when she was only eight years old: 'He was a slender, shy man with tremendous vivacity, peering out at the world short-sightedly through small, steel-rimmed spectacles. Although there were only about twelve of us in the class, he got tremendously excited conducting us, willing us to come in on time and insisting on very clear enunciation.'

He always aimed at letting his pupils sing some of the music that he himself was passionately fond of. 'I find the question of getting music for girls' schools perfectly hopeless,' he complained to a friend. 'I get reams of twaddle sent me periodically, and that is all the publishers seem to think is suitable for girls. So I have had some Di Lasso lithographed for St. Paul's.'

By this time he was also teaching grown-ups in evening classes at the Passmore Edwards Settlement in central London. Here he conducted the choir and orchestra in the first performances in England of two of Bach's cantatas, as well as the first complete performance of the 'Peasant' cantata.

It was in 1907 that he was appointed Musical Director at Morley College, which was then next door to the Old Vic in the Waterloo Road. The college had been founded in the late nineteenth century 'to promote the advanced study by men and women belonging to the working classes of subjects not directly connected with any handicraft, trade or business'. The list of students' occupations during his first few years there included: '1 Hackney Driver, 4 Piano Tuners, 2 Bakers, 2 Hotel Porters, 2 Lift Attendants, 3 Office Boys, 7 Schoolmasters, 1 Brewer's Assistant, 1 Engine Driver, 1 Seaman, 392 Clerks, 1 Cricket Bat Maker, 4 Embroideresses, 4 Police Constables, 1 Lady's Maid and 1 Tram Conductor.'

He never turned anyone away from a class, as long as they were prepared to work hard. His first Morley orchestra consisted of two violins, one flute, three clarinets with sharp pitch instruments, a cornet, and a piano. Four years after this, both the choir and orchestra had grown and flourished to such an extent that they were able to give the first concert performance since 1697 of Purcell's *Fairy Queen*. There were no orchestral parts available, so he asked the publisher's permission for the members of his Morley harmony class to copy them out in their spare time. It took them nearly eighteen months, and it was

ROYAL VICTORIA HALL,

WATERLOO ROAD, S.E.

PROGRAMME OF
CONCERT PERFORMANCE

OF

"The Fairy Queen"

OF

Henry Purcell

BY

The Music Students of Morley College,

On SATURDAY, JUNE 10th, 1911, at 8 p.m.

Under the direction of GUSTAV VON HOLST.

The full score of this work was lost shortly after Henry Purcell's death in 1695. It was recently discovered and the Purcell Society published it. By their permission, the Students of Morley College copied the entire Vocal and Orchestral Parts (1,500 pages).

COPYISTS—

J. Buckingham ⎫
C. Burke   ⎬ Principals.

M. Arrigoni	J. Harrison	N. Ramsden
J. Boomer	E. Hoare	A. Zimmerman
L. Boomer	S. Keating	C. Renouf
F. Burrell	H. Wootton	M. Riedtmann
L. Daniels	J. Kerslake	E. M. C. Soames
A. Elston	V. Lasker	R. Shapcott
A. Emberson	W. Lockett	C. Thompson
N. English	W. Newell	J. Westwood
R. Hamilton	W. Oldis	

PROGRAMME ... ... ONE PENNY.

All applications for Tickets should be made to Miss Sheepshanks, Vice-Principal, Morley College for Working Men and Women, Waterloo Road, S.E.

Boxes £1 1s. Balcony Stalls (Reserved) 2/6.
Unreserved Seats 1/6, 1/- and 6d.

characteristic of him that he insisted on the copyists' names being printed in the programme. Some years later, a journalist wrote an account of a typical Morley rehearsal:

> I had asked the conductor what was being prepared for the next concert. 'We're doing Beethoven's *Choral Fantasia* using a new translation by a Morleyite. Then we're doing three choruses from the Bach *B minor Mass*, Brahms' *Song of Destiny*, and a part-song by a member of the advanced harmony class: we always do something by a student at our concerts.' Before the rehearsal began, he talked to the singers and players for a few minutes about the music. 'Just one thing about the end of the Fantasia. You remember the convention of "the endless ending"?' (He played the formula on the piano: Tonic, Submediant, Subdominant, Dominant, repeated *ad lib*.) 'Well, it's just what Beethoven does for his Coda here. Of course, it's deplorable, but people unconsciously conform to the convention of their day, and Beethoven's audience never thought any the worse of him for giving them what they expected. And—there are probably things which *we* are doing today about which, in a hundred years, people will wonder how we *could* go on repeating such worn-out stuff. And now, we'll start on the Bach.' The chorus was 'on the whole, good'. He then asked me: 'What would you like us to do now? The Brahms? Certainly.' He turned to the performers—'We'll take the *Song of Destiny* next.' There was a fluttering of copies, and the conductor wheeled round again to his visitor. 'Did you see that? Their faces fell! Some of them don't like Brahms—they'd like to go on singing Bach all night! And to tell you the truth—' (Here he told me the truth.) '*Ha!* But I always do learn from my pupils!'

He hated all textbooks on harmony. 'The best textbook for teaching composition', he once told a critic, 'is the one we use at St. Paul's— Walter de la Mare's *Peacock Pie*.' And he hated compulsory examinations in music. He used to quote Samuel Butler's advice on education: 'Never learn anything until the not knowing it has come to be a nuisance to you.' This always worked very well in his exciting, unorthodox lessons. Nothing that mattered was ever neglected. When his pupils were asked during a rehearsal to fill in a missing clarinet or viola part on the piano, it immediately became an intolerable nuisance not to be able to transpose or to play in the C clef.

Teaching brought him a regular income, and he was now able to afford

Holst in his music room at Barnes, 1911

a house to live in. His wife was excellent at making a home really comfortable. She had begun with their tiny week-end cottage in the Isle of Sheppey, furnishing it with chintz-covered packing cases and with bits of pottery she had found on a market-stall in one of the narrow back-streets of Hammersmith. Later on, they rented a small Regency house at Barnes, overlooking the river. The music-room at the top of the house had a wonderful view from its three windows, and it was a quiet place for composing, as there was very little traffic in those days. This was the first home that I knew, and my earliest recollections were of hearing him play tunes for me to dance to.

His 'double life' as a teacher and a composer must have been exhausting, for the journeys between Barnes and Dulwich took up many

33

hours of the week, and at the end of his hard day's work at one of his schools he had to go straight on to Morley College to conduct the evening classes. Some of his friends were worried that he had so little time for his own music, and his Sanskrit teacher Patsy Bode even went so far as to send him a birthday letter wishing him 'all the good things of this earth, chiefly the extermination of schoolgirls from your life'. But he would never hear a word against teaching as a profession. He used to say: 'The vast majority of great artists of the world have been teachers—usually very good ones. Of course they grumbled when too much time had to be spent in teaching or when their pupils were more stupid than usual. Who wouldn't? But this is very different from *despising* teaching.' And he told a friend that writing music for his pupils to sing or play was something that meant a great deal to him. 'In spite of the obvious drawbacks of having to teach six hundred girls every week,' he said, 'I consider that I have learnt as much through my school teaching as I did as a trombone player in the Carl Rosa and the Scottish Orchestra.'

V Folk tunes and plainsong

It was in December 1903 that Vaughan Williams began collecting traditional English folk songs in the Essex village of Ingrave. They were sung to him by a seventy-four-year-old retired farm-worker called Mr. Pottipher, who, when asked where the tunes came from, replied: 'If you can get the words, the Almighty sends you a tune.'

These songs were a revelation to Holst. Until then, he had thought of folk songs as being either Irish or Scottish. But these newly-discovered English tunes were more beautiful than any he had yet heard. He was fascinated by all that Vaughan Williams and the other collectors could tell him, and he encouraged his pupils to listen to any songs they happened to hear while they were on holiday in the country. He met the great folk song collector Cecil Sharp, and invited him to give illustrated talks to the students at the Passmore Edwards Settlement. Sharp showed him several of the morris dance tunes he had recently been finding in Cotswold villages, and Holst remembered that when he was a small child in Cheltenham he had once heard a fiddle being played in the street and he had looked out of the window and seen men dancing with sticks in their hands and jingling bells tied to their legs and bright-coloured ribbons dangling from their hats.

Cecil Sharp was planning to publish several books of 'Folk Songs of England', with piano accompaniments to the tunes, and he asked Holst to arrange a volume of songs from Hampshire. He also gave him the idea of writing an orchestral piece founded on Somerset folk songs. The result was *A Somerset Rhapsody*, which begins with an oboe playing Holst's favourite traditional tune, 'It's a rosebud in June'. He told one of his friends that the form of *A Somerset Rhapsody* 'grew out of a suggestion of a pastoral countryside becoming filled with human activities but surviving them all.'

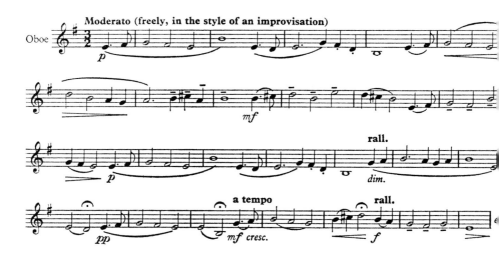

As a result of arranging so many folk songs, his own music became simpler and more direct: in his orchestral *Two Songs without Words*, written in 1906, the opening solo for unaccompanied clarinet might almost be a traditional tune. In his harmonies he managed to get rid of nearly all those chromatic sequences that had cluttered up so much of his music during the years when he had imitated Wagner. Now, at last, he was free to find his own way of expressing himself.

Country Song from *Two Songs without Words*

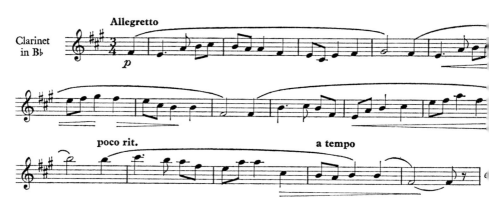

Tune from *Marching Song* from *Two Songs without Words*

One of his aims was to discover what he called 'the musical idiom of the English language'. He wanted to write tunes that would feel 'at one with the words'. Here folk songs helped him more than anything else, for their words and tunes seemed to have grown together, inseparably. His 1907 settings of medieval poems in the *Four Old English Carols* have a dancing liveliness that he had never known during the Christmasses when he was a choirboy at All Saints, Cheltenham.

His friend Vaughan Williams, who had first taught him about folk songs, was also able to teach him about plainsong when he showed him the tunes he had chosen for *The English Hymnal*, which he was then editing. There were traditional carols and seventeenth-century metrical psalm tunes to take the place of some of the most sentimental of the Victorian melodies. And there were plainsong hymns in the English Sarum tradition which had not been sung in churches since before the Reformation. It was the influence of plainsong that helped him to write his 1912 setting of *Psalm 86*.

From *Psalm 86*, the first of *Two Psalms*

38

Holst's love of plainsong hymns lasted throughout his life. He knew that this freely-flowing music was more important than a mere antique survival: it was gloriously alive and it belonged not only to the past but also to the present time and possibly to the future.

'Pange lingua' from The English Hymnal

VI Thaxted and the Whitsun festivals

'Walking always sets me thinking of new tunes,' Holst once told a friend. It was his favourite way of spending a short holiday whenever he could manage to get one. A five-day walk in the winter of 1913 through villages in north-west Essex happened to lead him to the small town of Thaxted, with its medieval houses and its magnificent church on the top of a hill. He liked the place so much that soon afterwards he brought me and my mother there and made it his home. Our 300-year-old thatched cottage was in Monk Street, about a mile from Thaxted. It stood high above the surrounding cornfields and meadows and willow trees, with a view of the church spire in the distance. It was so quiet that we could hear the bees in the dark red clover beyond the garden hedge. We could watch the meadow-grass being scythed, and in the cornfields we saw the farmer sowing the seed by hand, scattering it in the breeze as he strode up and down. The only traffic along what is now the main road was the carrier's cart which stopped every few hundred yards to pick up parcels and passengers on Wednesday afternoons: on the other days, people walked.

When the First World War began in 1914, the neighbours were suspicious of a stranger with a 'von' in his name. Several of them went to complain to the police, saying: 'He takes long walks about the country and was recently questioning some of the cottage women who were drawing water from a well.' The police, however, merely noted in their report: 'Many rumours are current about this man, but nothing can be traced against him.'

Meanwhile, Holst had already made friends with the singers in the church choir, who spoke of him affectionately as 'our Mr. Von'. Their socialist vicar, Conrad Noel, had taught them to sing plainsong during the Sunday services, and to process round the church on saints' days carrying lighted candles and bunches of flowers and brilliantly-

Thaxted church,
the north porch

coloured banners, while singing tunes from *The English Hymnal*. Like some other choirs in the eastern counties, the singers were inclined to half-close their mouths, as if to keep out the cold north-east winds. At Conrad Noel's request, Holst worked hard to improve the sound they made. (A scribbled reminder in one of his notebooks says: '2 boxes of voice lozenges for Thaxted singers'.) He also helped them with their sight-reading, and taught them to sing music by Byrd and other great English composers of the sixteenth century.

Thaxted church was such a perfect place for music-making that he asked if he might bring his singers and players from Morley College and St. Paul's Girls' School to join the Thaxted choir in an informal festival of music by Bach, Palestrina and Purcell. This was not the sort of

41

festival where an audience pays for tickets to go and listen to a performance: the programme at Thaxted was sung and played as part of the church service, and the only listeners were the congregation.

No one who was there at that 1916 festival will ever forget it. One of the players described it in the *Morley Magazine*:

> This has been the first musical festival at Thaxted, and we look forward most ardently to its return year by year. Mr. von Holst's choir and orchestra, consisting of Morleyites and Paulinas, arrived on the Saturday and were joined by the Thaxted singers for a rehearsal in the church. Whit Sunday was grey and showery: by 9.45 a.m. the singers and players were in their places in the Becket Chapel, almost hidden from the congregation by a carved screen.
>
> The church made an impression which will never be forgotten; at intervals bars of sunlight struck down through the great windows and lit up the pillars and hangings in golden patches; here and there on the stone floor stood great earthenware jars filled with larkspurs, peonies and beech boughs; and, high up among the vaulting, swallows darted in and out. It was one of the most beautiful services we shall ever take part in. Both choir and orchestra felt satisfied when they saw their conductor's face.
>
> Whit Monday made no pretences, but rained steadily all day. On both afternoons Mrs. von Holst entertained the musicians at Monk Street Cottage for tea; driven indoors by the rain they resorted at once to music—Elizabethan love songs, rounds and part-songs. On Monday evening we were invited by Mr. Noel to a Garden Party at the vicarage; owing to the downpour it was held in the dining-room— a varied and festive evening, beginning with folk songs and morris dances by the Thaxted singers, which they vainly tried to teach us till the house shook to its foundations—then a melodrama in the barn— and finally more dancing. By Tuesday the last musicians had left, and so ended this wonderful festival.

When it was over, Holst wrote a long, excited letter to his friend W. G. Whittaker, who was an enthusiastic choir-trainer:

> Our musical festival at Thaxted was a feast—an orgy. Four whole days of perpetual singing and playing, either properly arranged in the church or impromptu in various houses or still more impromptu in ploughed fields during thunderstorms.

Thaxted church, showing the organ that Holst played

He also wrote:

I realise now why the bible insists on heaven being a place (I should call it a condition) where people sing and *go on singing*. We kept it up at Thaxted about fourteen hours a day. The reason why we didn't do more is that we were not capable mentally or physically of realising heaven any further.

Of course, it's no use writing this. If you've had four days of perpetual music you've learnt it already, and if you haven't it's about as sensible as describing the B minor Mass to a deaf man.

Music, being identical with heaven, isn't a thing of momentary thrills, or even hourly ones. It's a condition of eternity.

43

From *Four Songs for Voice and Violin*

It was during that Whit Sunday, in an interval between services, that he happened to go into the church when a woman was walking up and down the empty aisles, singing a wordless song as she played the open strings of her violin. The sound was so astonishing in that resonant, spacious building that it gave him the idea of writing his *Four Songs for Voice and Violin*. In these settings of medieval religious poems he felt that at last he had learnt how to write 'a tune at one with the words'.

This have I done for my true love

Allegretto

Soprano solo or semichorus

To - mor - row shall be my danc - ing day, I would my true_ love did so chance To_ see the le - gend of my play, To call my true love to the dance, Sing oh my love, Oh my love, my love, my love, This have I done for my true love. Then was I born of a Vir - gin pure, Of her I took flesh - ly sub-stance: *etc.*

He was also writing music for the Thaxted choir to sing, including the cheerful Festival Chorus 'Our church-bells in Thaxted' and the carol *This have I done for my true love*, which he always referred to as 'The Dancing Day'. Conrad Noel had discovered the words of this carol in an old book of verses and had copied them out and pinned them up on the notice-board just inside the church door. As soon as Holst read them, he knew that this image of the redemption of mankind through 'the General Dance' was just what he had been waiting for. His original tune for the carol suited the words so inevitably that he often had to explain to people that it was not a traditional folk song. He thought it his 'best thing' for unaccompanied voices.

'The Dancing Day' was sung at the third Whitsun festival in 1918. This was the last of his festivals to be held in Thaxted. He continued to help the church choir whenever he had a free weekend at home, but the Whitsun tradition was carried on, year after year, in other churches and in cathedrals.

At the fourth Whitsun he had to manage without any of his London pupils, for by then he was working in Constantinople (now known as Istanbul). He had been considered unfit for any active war-work, owing to his neuritis and his short sight. But in the autumn of 1918 he was sent to the Middle East for nine months by the Young Men's Christian Association, as Musical Organizer in their educational work among the troops who were soon to be demobilized. (It was because of this appointment that he gave up the 'von' in his name.)

'The thing promises to be a great success,' he wrote from Salonica, 'and I am overwhelmed both by the quantity and the quality of the men who want music here. Occasionally, but not often, I am also overwhelmed—or partly so—by the difficulties.'

In the spring of 1919 the authorities sent him to Constantinople, and from there he wrote: 'I am trying to combine a musical competition with a massed concert of choirs and orchestras on Whit Monday which will be repeated every night of the week. I have put some Byrd and a lot of madrigals and folk songs down in the competition, so that if it comes off it may convince people here that there's something in British music after all. Anyhow, it's worth trying. Though at times I think it cannot possibly take place! And my only reason for hoping that it may is that I have felt like that over previous Whitsuntides. But this is much more difficult, and I have no resourceful Morleyites to fall back on.'

A resourceful army captain who was a trained musician came to his rescue, and afterwards gave an account of what had happened:

I was ordered to report for temporary duty at G.H.Q. Constantinople. A French hospital ship landed me late in the evening and I was told to go immediately to see Holst. I found him in a state of great agitation; he was evidently relieved to see me. 'Thank God you have come!' he said. 'I was in despair! Tomorrow morning we have Musical Competitions for the whole of the Army of the Black Sea. Some of the competitors are coming a thousand miles. We have bands, choirs, composers, violinists, pianists and singers, coming from as far away as Batoum and Baku, and *you* are the judge!'

The Competitions were followed by an 'all-British' concert. I was not expecting to take any share, but at the last moment he said to me: 'Take charge of the "invisible" choir which will start singing *Sumer is icumen in* a long way off and will approach the main chorus gradually. Then lead them away so as to make an opposite effect at the end.' When this was over he said: 'Now hurry down to the orchestra, where there is a spare viola waiting for you!' When the orchestral piece was finished he turned to me and said: 'Go up to the choir and sing second tenor in the Byrd *Three-part Mass*.' No sooner was that done than he told me to accompany a singer who was going to sing the song which had won a prize in the composition class. I was unprepared for this role of quick-change artist, but it was typical of Holst. He liked people to *do* things.

Half-way through that Whitsun week, which was Holst's 'final effort' in the Middle East before returning to England, he wrote to his wife:

On the whole our musical competition has been a success, although not a brilliant one. But it has left a deep impression on many, especially the choir, and that is the main point.

'A Chime for Homecoming' is this year's Whitsuntide version of 'Our church-bells in Thaxted'.

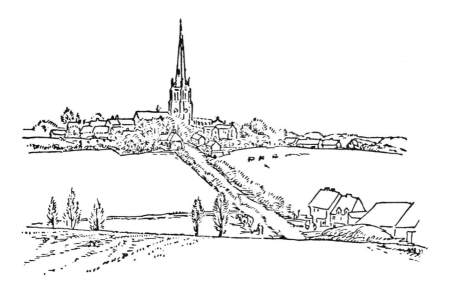

VII The Planets *and* The Hymn of Jesus

A few weeks before he had left England for the Middle East, Holst was able to hear a private performance of the biggest work he had yet written. This was *The Planets*. The performance was a present from his rich friend Balfour Gardiner, a generous patron who had already helped him on many occasions, paying for his unknown works to be performed at Queen's Hall, commissioning him to orchestrate music when he was short of money, and inviting him for holidays when he was feeling tired and discouraged.

It was while he was with Balfour Gardiner in Spain, in the spring of 1913, that he met the young author Clifford Bax and learnt about astrology. He wrote to a friend soon afterwards, saying: 'I only study things that suggest music to me. That's why I worried at Sanskrit. Then recently the character of each planet suggested lots to me, and I have been studying astrology fairly closely. It's a pity we make such a fuss about these things. On one side there is nothing but abuse and ridicule, with the natural result that when one is brought face to face with overwhelming proofs there is a danger of going to the other extreme. Whereas, of course, everything in this world—writing a letter for instance—is just one big miracle. Or rather, the universe itself is one.'

The music that the character of each planet had suggested to him was eventually to become a symphonic suite with seven movements: *Mars*, the Bringer of War; *Venus*, the Bringer of Peace; *Mercury*, the Winged Messenger; *Jupiter*, the Bringer of Jollity; *Saturn*, the Bringer of Old Age; *Uranus*, the Magician; and *Neptune*, the Mystic. He began work on *The Planets* during the summer of 1914, and he had finished the first sketch of *Mars* before the outbreak of war in August. Many people have taken it for granted that the music owed its fierce cruelty to the horror of mechanized fighting. But *Mars* was not a comment on the war: it was a prophecy. When his friends used to ask him about it he said: 'I had the whole of Mars fixed in my mind before August, and the only planet I was quite certain I was thinking about in the second half of 1914 was Venus—the bringer of peace.'

Mars was begun in the cottage at Thaxted. He wrote the other movements in his sound-proof teaching room in the newly-built music-wing at St. Paul's Girls' School. This was where he was to write nearly all his works during the remaining twenty years of his life. He used to look forward to what he called the 'spell' of his room, where he could shut himself up at the end of a busy week and forget everything except what he was composing. During school hours he could snatch only an occasional twenty minutes before he had to go on teaching. (One of his

His sound-proof room at St. Paul's Girls' School

1915 harmony pupils remembered going for a lesson one day with another pupil and being greeted with the words: 'Come in and listen to what I've just finished writing.' It was *Saturn*, and the three of them tried it over on the piano.)

Weekends and holidays were the only times when he could really get on with his own work, which is why it took him over two years to finish *The Planets*. His neuritis was troubling him a good deal and he would have found it impossible to complete the 198 pages of the large full score without the help of two music teachers at St. Paul's, his friends Vally Lasker and Nora Day, whom he used to call his 'scribes'.

While he was working on *The Planets* he felt sure he would have to wait many years before getting a chance to hear it. 'I remember so well', wrote one of his composition pupils, 'that when he first introduced me to *Jupiter* he said that it was written for a vast orchestra which no one would be able to afford in war-time.' But in September 1918 Balfour Gardiner hired the Queen's Hall, London, for an invited audience and engaged the Queen's Hall Orchestra to sight-read the new work under the twenty-nine-year-old conductor Adrian Boult. The orchestral parts had to be written out at short notice. Someone must have mentioned that there were highly skilled German musicians in London who were temporarily out of work, for in Holst's 1918 notebook there is the pencil-led suggestion: 'prisoners copy Planet parts Islington Internment Camp?' On the morning of Sunday, 29th September the orchestra rehearsed for just under two hours and then played the work straight through. The two or three hundred friends and fellow musicians who had come to listen in the half-dark auditorium realized that this was no ordinary occasion: the music was unlike anything they had ever heard before. They found the clamour of *Mars* almost unbearable after having lived through four years of a war that was still going on. The cool to-and-fro of the chords in *Venus* had a balanced tranquillity that had not yet become a familiar device. The scurry of *Mercury* was breathlessly exciting; I can remember, during the tuning up in the rehearsal, seeing and hearing all those violinists frantically trying to decide on the right fingering for their rapid high quavers. *Jupiter* was thoroughly happy, without any of the false associations that were afterwards to link the big tune to the words of a patriotic hymn. In *Saturn* the middle-aged listeners in the audience felt they were growing older and older as the slow, relentless tread came nearer. (As I was then only eleven I was not yet able to understand why the composer thought *Saturn* the best of the seven

movements.) The magical moment in *Uranus* was when all the noise was suddenly blotted out, leaving a quietness that seemed as remote as the planet in the sky. It was the end of *Neptune* that was more memorable than anything else at that first performance. Hearing the voices of the hidden choir growing fainter and fainter, it was impossible to know where the sound ended and the silence began. Holst had been very careful about placing the singers so as to get the right effect. Several years later, when he asked me to play the cues for his chorus rehearsals, I found out how he managed it. The singers began by standing out of sight in a box next to the Queen's Hall organ. They were able to look at the conductor through a narrow gap between the curtains. After about three bars they slowly turned round and walked down a corridor, watching the beat of a sub-conductor, who led them into a room at the far end, where a door was open to receive them. They walked the whole length of this room while someone gradually closed the door, and they went on singing until the applause of the audience told them that their voices were no longer audible. Holst used to make them rehearse this over and over again: any shoes that squeaked had to be taken off, and the door had to be shut absolutely silently. He was a very practical composer, and he always knew exactly what he wanted.

He was not able to be at the first public performance of *The Planets*, as he was then in the Middle East. Unfortunately only five of the seven movements were played on this occasion, and it was not until the nineteen-twenties that the whole work was played in public. He hated incomplete performances, though on several occasions he had to agree to conduct shortened versions of only three or four movements. He particularly disliked having to finish with *Jupiter*, to make 'a happy ending', for, as he said, 'in the real work the end is not happy at all'.

51

Before long, however, concert organizers realized that they could risk the expense of the complete work, for their audiences were agreeing with Vaughan Williams that 'Holst has something to tell us that only he can say, and he has found the only way of saying it'.

Soon after he had finished scoring *The Planets* he began thinking about his next work, *The Hymn of Jesus*. He had been searching for words of 'dancing hymns' ever since writing *This have I done for my true love*, and the search led him in the summer of 1917 to a second-century Greek hymn from the apocryphal Acts of St. John. The scene is described in detail: 'He bade us therefore make as it were a ring, holding one another's hands, and himself standing in the midst he said: Answer Amen unto me. He began then to sing an hymn and to say: *Glory be to thee, Father.* And we, going about in a ring, answered him: *Amen.*' The 'going about in a ring' was undoubtedly a dance, for at the end of the hymn the text says: 'Then, having danced these things with us, the Lord went forth.'

While Holst was working at his translation of the text he must often have been reminded of 'The Dancing Day', especially at the triumphant line: 'All things join in the dance!' He must also have been reminded of his Sanskrit studies, for he had long ago read in the Bhagavad Gita:

> *I am Knowledge, that brilliant lamp . . .*
> *Whatever path men travel*
> *Is my path!*

And now, in the apocryphal hymn, he was discovering the words:

> *To you who gaze, a lamp am I,*
> *To you who fare, the way.*

'I'm trying to set the "Hymn of Jesus" out of the Apocryphal Gospels,' he wrote to Whittaker, 'for two mixed choirs, a third choir of female voices and an orchestra of rather more than a dozen (in other words, a damned big one). Incidentally, I'm trying to learn Greek so as to read it in the original, so altogether I'm very happy. Oh my friend, why do we waste our lives trying to teach! (Don't trouble to answer—I've already thought of several answers.)'

For his translation, he copied out the original Greek, and then, with the help of his composition pupil Jane Joseph, he wrote the approximate pronunciation and the literal English meaning of each word before making his own version.

The Hymn of Jesus is unlike any other English religious music. It made an overwhelming impression on the listeners. One of them wrote to Holst, saying: 'It completely bowls me over. Your presentation of it is the poem, the whole poem and nothing but the poem. It couldn't have been done before—and it can't be done again. It's a blessed abiding fact. If anybody doesn't like it, he doesn't like life.' Another listener wrote, long afterwards: 'I shall never forget the rehearsals at the Royal College of Music for one of the first performances. To us who were young then and eager for something that would lift us out of the rut of common experience, this very new music came first as a shock, then as a revelation.'

υπακουε δε μου τη χορεια
upahoae de mou te khoreia
attend   of me   the dancing

(14) ΙΔΕ ΣΕΑΥΤΟΝ ΕΝ ΕΜΟΙ ΛΑΛΟΥΝΤΙ ΚΑΙ ΙΔΩΝ ὅ πρασσω
Ide seauton en emoi lalounti kai idon o prasso
see thyself in me talking and what I do
(know)   who speaks   having seen

Τα μυστηρια μου σιγα
ta mysteria mou siga
the mysteries let me have silence

VIII *The disadvantages of success*

When Holst conducted the first performance of *The Hymn of Jesus* in March 1920 the Queen's Hall audience clapped so loudly and so persistently that the concert organizers felt embarrassed at having to refuse the request for it to be encored. 'I'm sending you the press notices of the H. of J.', Holst wrote to a friend. 'It has made me realise the truth of "Woe to you when all men speak well of you." I feel that something is wrong somewhere, but don't know where or how.'

He had once said to Clifford Bax: 'Some day I expect you will agree with me that it's a great thing to be a failure. If nobody likes your work, you have to go on just for the sake of the work. And you're in no danger of letting the public make you repeat yourself. Every artist ought to pray that he may not be "a success". If he's a failure he stands a good chance of concentrating upon the best work of which he's capable.'

By the end of 1920 there was no longer any doubt that *The Planets* was also a success. At the first public performance, when the work was played without *Venus* or *Neptune*, some of the listeners were not sure about it. But at the first complete performance 'the entire audience rose with tumultuous applause'. And not long after this *The Times* was saying: 'Mr Gustav Holst seems to have achieved the position, rare for an Englishman, of being a really popular composer.'

It was a position that he would gladly have avoided. He hated having to waste time on social engagements instead of getting on with his own work. And he loathed all the fuss of publicity in the press. Genuine criticism was a very different matter. He used to say: 'The critical faculty is as important, as necessary, as divine, as the imaginative one: it is impossible to overrate the real critic.' He also said: 'All artists must be critics, for art implies selection. And a sympathetic critic's disapproval is the most interesting and stimulating experience I know.' But by now there were so many press reporters who seemed to care about nothing except getting hold of some sort of a 'story'. ('I was a bit annoyed', he complained, 'when certain newspapers dragged in bits about Zeus in *The Planets*: the legends about Greek and Roman gods have nothing to do with it.')

Worst of all were the reporters who wanted to interview him. Occasionally they managed to give their readers a glimpse of what he looked like: '. . . that rather short, thick-set, fair man with a high forehead and glasses, to be seen proceeding hurriedly but firmly along the Waterloo Road'. There is a good description of him giving a lecture: '. . . now clutching the lapel of his coat, now picking words out of the air with his left hand, now pointing an accusing finger at the window'. And there is one excellent phrase in a gossip column where, under the unpromising heading of 'What struck me most about Gustav Holst', the writer says: 'The impression he gives that he is walking on air when he is listening to good music.' Such glimpses, however, are rare. Most of the reporters were obviously defeated by his stubborn resistance, like the unfortunate man who wrote: 'Mr Holst quite rightly refuses to be drawn from his proper task of composing music into the noise of public argument. "No, no" he said to me, speaking with the utmost rapidity, "I never answer criticisms. If I once started I should have to give up everything else." '

He would have liked to have said 'No, no,' to all photographers, except for the two or three who were his friends. The photographs in this book were taken by people he enjoyed being with. But when he was interrupted by a newspaper photographer, the sullen droop of his expression showed his dislike of publicity.

There were very few honours that he accepted. He refused every offer of an honorary degree, and one of his closest friends received a postcard saying: 'I'm sorry I can't do what you ask but I've made a strict rule never to be patron or vice-president etc. etc. to anything or anybody.' This strict rule of his was not just the result of having immersed himself in Hindu philosophy when he was young. It was also the result of the practical way he planned his working hours from week to week and from year to year: he knew that one honorary doctorate would lead to another, and he could not risk losing any of the precious days that were to be left free for composition.

Success brought him more money to live on, but this also had its disadvantages. He used to say: 'Music-making as a means of getting money is hell.' This was not a 'moral' opinion: it was the belief of a hard-working professional who knew by experience that life would be intolerable if his heart were not in the music he was doing all day every day.

He cared very little about material possessions. The only personal belongings that he treasured were Beethoven's tuning-fork, which was sent to him by an unknown admirer, and the key that let him into his sound-proof music-room at St. Paul's Girls' School during week-ends and holidays. The things in life that gave him most pleasure were things that could not be bought with money. He enjoyed long walks on the Cotswold hills, or in beech woods, or across open moors. He enjoyed looking at pictures and wandering round cathedrals. And he enjoyed leisurely conversations with his friends, either in one of the London parks, or in 'The George' at Hammersmith Broadway.

56 *Holst and Vaughan Williams on a walking holiday*

There seemed to be less time for these pleasures during the early nineteen-twenties, for success was making his life so much more complicated.

When his new comic opera, *The Perfect Fool*, was produced on the opening night of the 1923 London season of the British National Opera Company, it was advertised as if it were by far the most important musical event of the year. After the first performance, a sympathetic critic wrote: '*The Perfect Fool* may not turn out to be Gustav Holst's work of firmest permanency, but its production at Covent Garden on May 14th made for a notoriety that *The Planets* and *The Hymn of Jesus* had missed by miles. We must take the world as we find it, and we may smile that this burst of notoriety descends on a man who, more than almost anyone, is indifferent to applause.'

The first-night audience at *The Perfect Fool* was puzzled by the light-hearted parodies of Wagner and nineteenth-century Italian opera. They liked the ballet music, with its brilliantly orchestrated dances for the spirits of earth, water and fire. And they liked the beautiful round sung by three girls drawing water from a well. But most of the time they felt uncomfortable, not quite knowing when they were supposed to laugh.

Round for three voices from *The Perfect Fool*

A few months later, his listeners were again puzzled: this time it was at the first performance of his *Fugal Concerto*. They had come hoping to hear something that would remind them of *The Planets*. But they were given a short, delicately-poised study in counterpoint, founded on the eighteenth-century style of a chamber concerto.

There was certainly no danger of his letting the public make him repeat himself. He went his own way, quietly concentrating on the best work of which he was capable. And, fortunately for his peace of mind, his position as 'a really popular composer' only lasted a very few years.

IX   Overwork and recovery

In October 1923 the Queen's Hall was sold out twice in one week when Holst was conducting his own music. This was the climax of his popularity, and it happened to coincide with the beginning of an illness which was due to the effects of concussion. He told one of his friends: 'I was obviously overworked by 1922 and was making plans to do less teaching. But in February 1923 while conducting at Reading University College I fell off the platform backwards on to my head. It was not serious but apparently I did not lay up long enough.' This accident upset him at the time, but the effects of the concussion soon wore off and he was allowed to visit the University of Michigan as lecturer and conductor. He enjoyed his three months in America, and he was looking well when he came back to England. By the autumn, however, he began to have pains in the back of his head, and he felt so weary that he could hardly bear the thought of all the work he had to do.

Throughout his life he had been used to the strain of long hours of work. But now that he was in his fiftieth year he had more work to get through than ever before. In addition to all his other teaching he was now on the staff of the Royal College of Music and the University College at Reading, training future professionals to be composers. This was a very different matter from the carefree amateur classes at Morley College, where his pupils 'made up rounds and then spent their lessons in singing them'. Remembering that when he himself had been at the Royal College of Music he had instinctively tried to please his professor, he was now anxious to prevent his pupils from writing nothing but imitations of his own music. He need not have worried, however, for he taught them to think for themselves, as well as to be practical.

Lecturing in public was now taking up much more of his time, and this was another cause of anxiety. 'I wish I could either abandon lecturing, or do it better,' he confessed to a friend. But here again he need not have

59

worried about it so much. His university lectures were always lively, and when he talked about the recently discovered masterpieces of sixteenth-century English music, his own excitement over his favourite madrigal composers and lutenist song-writers was so irresistible that his audiences felt equally excited.

The amount of conducting he was now having to do was an additional strain, particularly when his arm was feeling 'like a jelly overcharged with electricity'. With amateurs, he could spare himself by using his left arm for conducting, but he tried to avoid this with professional orchestras. Recording sessions were more tiring than anything he had yet had to endure. At his first pre-electric recording of *The Planets* the huge orchestra was packed into a room that was much too small; the string players were unable to draw out the full length of their bows for a crescendo and the superb solo horn player broke down thirteen times at the beginning of *Venus*, owing to the discomfort of not having enough air to breathe. When Holst got home after that session he was so exhausted that he was unable to walk upstairs.

A good deal of his time and energy had to be given to preparing his works for publication, and this robbed him of the hours when he should have been thinking about his next piece of music. This is a problem that faces all composers; the more they write, the more time they need for seeing that their works are accurately published. For Holst, the problem was worse than usual, because his sudden popularity had stirred the publishers to take more interest in him, and many of his earlier, little-known manuscript works were now unexpectedly in demand. He had to revise the *Two Songs without Words, Savitri*, the *St. Paul's Suite* and at least a dozen shorter works for publication at the same time as correcting the proofs of *The Planets* and *The Perfect Fool*. He would have liked to have had much longer for revising his earlier works, but there was no time to spare for them. When he looked at his engagement book for the spring of 1924, hoping to set aside a period for composing, he was faced with entries such as these:

Friday, 21 March	*Mars, Venus, Mercury, Jupiter* at Bradford, rehearse 3, midnight train
Saturday, 22 March	Queen's Hall, rehearse 10, concert 3, *Perfect Fool* ballet
Sunday, 23 March	Queen's Hall, rehearse 10, concert 3·30, *Uranus, Neptune*

A lane near
Thaxted

The perpetual worry of having too much to do kept him awake at night. He felt so wretched, day after day, that at last he knew he was defeated. His doctor told him that he must cancel all his professional engagements during 1924 and live alone in Thaxted.

The Thaxted home was no longer the cottage at Monk Street: it was a square house in the middle of the town. The walled garden behind the house was sheltered from the wind, and it was quiet, for there was still very little traffic on the roads. Walking along those familiar fieldpaths and lanes, his strength gradually came back to him, and he soon began to feel better. Before long, he was well enough to work at his *Choral Symphony* on Keats' poems.

61

He was now able to live what he called 'the life of a real composer'. It was the first time he had ever had the chance to work at his own music hour after hour, every day of the week. 'It has been wonderful', he wrote to a friend, 'to sit in the garden and to watch the symphony grow up alongside of the flowers and vegetables, and then to find that it is done!'

He had made his own selection of poems by Keats, disregarding the complaints of some of his literary friends who had been dismayed to come across the *Ode on a Grecian Urn* next to such 'doggerel' as *Fancy* and *Folly's Song*. As usual, he knew just what he wanted for his music. And throughout these contrasting poems there is a clear thread of thought linking each movement: it is the conviction that the poet, in the strength of his imagination, can triumph over the shortcomings of material existence.

Extracts from the *Choral Symphony*

Soon after he had finished the *Choral Symphony* he began work on his new comic opera, *At the Boar's Head*, an 'interlude' founded on the Falstaff scenes in *Henry IV*. ('As the critics have decided that I can't write a libretto,' he explained to a friend, 'the words of my new opera are by Shakespeare.') He used to call it 'an opera that wrote itself', because he had discovered quite by chance that the words of one of the speeches happened to fit the tune of a seventeenth-century country dance I had shown him in Playford's collection. He began to explore other tunes, and before long he had written a whole opera with the help of anonymous English dances. 'My head is in a lovely chaos of the divine expletives of Doll and Pistol,' he told one of his composition pupils. 'Surely their quarrel is one of the wonders of the world. If there were any chance of my ever learning to express myself as Pistol does, I'd really consider the advisability of getting drunk. However, instead of doing so, I have concocted a brand new discord (I hope) for "I'll see her damned first".'

Early in 1925 he was well enough to go back to London. His doctor had ordered him to give up all teaching, except for a little work at St. Paul's Girls' School, but he was allowed to lecture and conduct. His hair had turned white and he had grown heavier; he no longer gave the impression of walking on air. He still had occasional headaches, and he found it difficult to bear the noise of London traffic or the clatter of conversation in a large crowd of people. This gave him an excuse for refusing the social engagements he so much disliked. And, as it happened, there were fewer invitations, for his popularity was dwindling.

At the Boar's Head disappointed its audiences. They felt almost as if they had been cheated because there were so few original tunes in the work, though there was one listener who pointed out that 'if anyone thinks that all he has to do to produce a similar work is to take down a volume of Shakespeare with one hand and a volume of Playford's tunes with the other and shake the two up together, he had just better try!'

The first London performance of the *Choral Symphony* went badly, and most of the listeners disliked the work. 'Holst's latest developments fill me with dismay,' wrote one critic. 'Holst presents the melancholy spectacle of a continuous and unrelieved decline,' wrote another.

A bad first performance is one of the most distressing things that can happen to a composer. But Holst knew that the symphony was as good as anything he had yet written. He was quite unmoved by the critics' disapproval. And, though he never spoke about it, I think he must have felt considerably relieved that there were fewer press photographers and no more gossip columns.

With less teaching to do, he had more time to see his friends and to write music for them. A visit to Robert Bridges' home in Oxford was combined with an informal first performance of his *Seven Bridges Part-Songs*: he took some of his pupils to sing and play to the poet, and it was one of the happiest afternoons he had ever known. ('I wonder if you agree with me', he once said, 'that music should either be done in a church or in someone's home. It was the Thaxted festivals that first made me realise it. For "personality" no longer counts for anything, and when that happens, music begins.')

Although he had had to give up teaching at Morley College he still met the students at Whitsun festivals, and in 1926 he wrote a choral ballet, *The Golden Goose*, for them to perform out of doors.

In the grounds of St. Paul's Girls' School, where The Golden Goose *was first performed*

Procession from *The Golden Goose*

Song from *The Coming of Christ*

Allegro moderato

Chorus and organ:

By wea - ry sta - ges The old world a - ges; By blood, by ra - ges, By pain - sown seeds. By fools and sa - ges, With death_ for wa - ges, Souls leave_ their ca - ges And Man does deeds. *etc.*

Whitsun 1928 was the Morleyites' most ambitious effort, for they performed his incidental music to John Masefield's play, *The Coming of Christ,* in the nave of Canterbury Cathedral. The Dean, Dr. George Bell, became one of Holst's best friends, and soon afterwards, when he had been made Bishop of Chichester, there were Whitsun festivals in his own cathedral.

By 1928, Holst was feeling much stronger. He was no longer upset by crowds of people. He was able to enjoy going for long walks with his friends. And he was able to listen to his *Moorside Suite* for brass band being played fifteen times on end, as the test piece in the Crystal Palace championship contest.

67

March from *A Moorside Suite*

People sometimes ask why he took the trouble to write commissioned works like this. But there was no question of 'trouble' about it. He thoroughly enjoyed writing music that had been asked for and that was needed for some special occasion.

It was in answer to a New York request for a commissioned orchestral piece that he wrote *Egdon Heath*, which he was quite sure was his best work.

69

X   Egdon Heath

Holst had first known Thomas Hardy's writings in the days when he was a student, and he had tried to set several of the poems for solo voice and piano while still earning his living as a trombone player. A few years later he ventured to send three of these manuscript songs to Hardy, who wrote him a generous letter of thanks, saying 'I think they are very beautiful (so far as I am a judge), and I hope you will publish them and make some profit by them, which I need hardly say would be entirely yours. If I can be of any help in doing it, please inform me.'

By the nineteen-twenties Hardy had become a friend, and Holst had learnt to know the Dorset landscape of the novels, particularly the stretch of country east of Dorchester which Hardy, in *The Return of the Native*, he referred to as 'the vast tract of unenclosed wild known as Egdon Heath'.

In a letter to an American friend, written from Dorchester on 11th August 1927, Holst said:

> Your gift of *The Return of the Native*, combined with a walk over Egdon Heath at Easter 1926 started my mind working, and I felt that according to my usual slow method I might write something in 1930 or thereabouts. However, a cable came last Easter from the New York Symphony Orchestra asking me to write something for them! With the result that my *Egdon Heath* was half done by the end of July, and last Friday I started walking here from Bristol via the Mendips, Wells and Sherbourne. I got here on Monday, and on Tuesday I had an unforgettable lunch and motor trip with Thomas Hardy himself, who showed me Melstock, Rainbarrow and Egdon in general. I've promised him to go up Rainbarrow by night. He is sorry I'm seeing it in summer weather, and wants me to come again in November.

MAX GATE.
DORCHESTER.

6 Aug. 1927

Dear Mr Holst:

We shall be delighted to see you on Tuesday next, & my wife says will you come to lunch at one o'clock.

I will not go into the news you give me of the musical creation you have contrived on Egdon Heath. I am sure it will be very striking. I accept the dedication with pleasure.

Sincerely yours
Thomas Hardy

Thomas Hardy's letter about Egdon Heath

One of the reasons that Hardy wished it had not been August was because he missed the subtle, characteristic sound of the 'worn whisper' of the winter wind blowing through the thousands of dry, shrivelled heath-flowers. Holst already knew this 'intermittent recitative' that 'brushed across the ear' so softly that it only just emerged from silence, and there is a passage in the music of *Egdon Heath* where the restless rustling of the strings is like a recollection of that wintry sound.

The mood of the music had grown out of a sentence in the opening chapter of *The Return of the Native*, where the heath is described as 'a place perfectly accordant with man's nature—neither ghastly, hateful, nor ugly: neither commonplace, unmeaning, nor tame; but, like man, slighted and enduring; and withal singularly colossal and mysterious in its swarthy monotony.'

While he was working on the music, Holst showed the manuscript to Vaughan Williams, who, at first, had his doubts about it. Several years later, in an article on Holst's music, he wrote:

> I remember once discussing *Egdon Heath* with him. I suggested that the very clearness of the melodic outlines of the piece were at variance with its atmospheric nature: indeed that less robust melody would have been more successful in impressionistic suggestion. Holst, on that occasion, lived up to his own maxim 'always ask for advice but never take it'. I am glad that he did so, for I now see that a less clear melody would have softened and thereby impaired the bleak grandeur of its outline.

In the full score, the words 'Homage to Thomas Hardy' are printed as a sub-title. Hardy had accepted the dedication, but he died before there was a chance of his hearing the music. The first European performance was in February 1928, at the Town Hall, Cheltenham. Holst conducted, and it went well. But the first London performance a few days later was disastrous. The concert organizers had put *Egdon Heath* as the second item on the programme, after the overture, and the foreign conductor was not used to Queen's Hall audiences. He made the fatal mistake of starting the orchestra before some of the late arrivals in the stalls had got into their places. The quiet, mysterious opening for muted double basses was inaudible: one could see the players' bowing arms moving slowly to and fro, but nothing could be heard through the buzz of conversation and the shuffle of feet. Those members of the audience who were already in their places glared at the late-comers and said '*ssshhh*', which added to the

The beginning of Egdon Heath

confusion. The guilty late-comers glared back, furious with the conductor for having started too soon, and even more furious with the composer for having written such a quiet opening. After this, the music had little chance of making an impression on those who had not yet seen the score. Most listeners found the work uncomfortably austere, and critics complained of its monotony.

'I am, of course, disappointed about the reception of *Egdon Heath,*' Holst wrote to his publisher. 'On the other hand I have my own very decided opinion on the work which prevents me from being as disappointed as I ought to be.'

He knew that it was his best work. This was where he felt most at home, in the vast solitude of Hardy's 'impersonal open ground'. And Hardy, if he could have heard this homage to him, would have recognized the mood of his own heath. 'Haggard Egdon', he had written in *The Return of the Native,* 'appealed to a subtler and scarcer instinct, to a more recently learnt emotion, than that which responds to the sort of beauty called charming and fair. The time seems near, if it has not actually arrived, when the chastened sublimity of a moor, a sea, or a mountain will be all of nature that is absolutely in keeping with the moods of the more thinking among mankind.'

73

XI   *The last five years*

Soon after the publication of *Egdon Heath* Holst had a letter from an old friend saying: 'I feel that you are getting a little beyond me. I am still in the primitive state where I need to be charmed by a certain superficial beauty. *You* have probably got at the roots of things, where this remains of little consequence, and I know you are too great an artist to have failed either in vision or realization. But I am fearful lest the price of it for you may mean a certain solitariness of soul, which even friends may be unable to comfort.'

The 'solitariness' was inevitable. Even Vaughan Williams, who was closer to him than any other friend, had confessed that he felt only a 'cold admiration' after hearing his *Choral Symphony*. 'I couldn't bear to think that I was going to "drift apart" from you musically speaking,' he had said to Holst on this occasion. They never drifted apart, but during the last five years of Holst's life there were other new works, including *Hammersmith*, which Vaughan Williams 'couldn't quite get hold of' at a first hearing.

Hammersmith was a Prelude and Scherzo which had been commissioned by the B.B.C. Military Band: Holst afterwards re-scored it for orchestra. 'As far as the work owes anything to outside influences,' he wrote, 'it is the result of living in Hammersmith for thirty-five years on and off and wanting to express my feelings for the place in music. There is no programme and no attempt to depict any person or incident. The only two things that I think were in my mind were (1) a district crowded with cockneys which would be overcrowded if it were not for the everlasting good humour of the people concerned, and (2) the background of the river, that was there before the crowd and will be there presumably long after, and which goes on its way largely unnoticed and apparently quite unconcerned.'

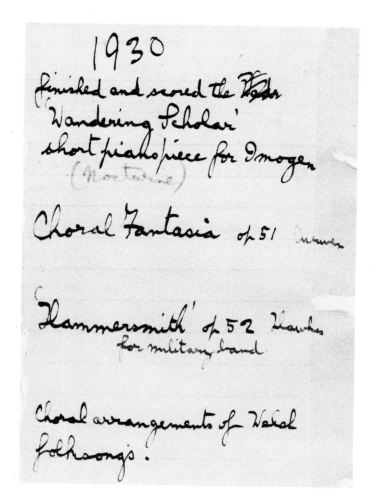

The 1930 page from Holst's list of compositions

In *Hammersmith* the contrast between the river-music and the crowd-music is unmistakably clear. The two moods, however, are allowed to overlap. Owing to the skill of his counterpoint he was able to achieve the 'unity of opposites' that he had already begun thinking about when he was a student.

75

Most of the listeners at the first performance of the orchestral version of *Hammersmith* found the river Prelude too slow, too quiet, too monotonous, and—like *Egdon Heath*—too uncomfortable.

They found his other 1930 commissioned work even more uncomfortable to listen to. This was the *Choral Fantasia*, written for the Three Choirs Festival at Gloucester Cathedral. He had taken the words from the *Ode to Music* which Robert Bridges wrote for Purcell's bicentenary in 1895. The work is like a requiem for poets and composers:

> *Rejoice, ye dead, where'er your spirits dwell,*
> *Rejoice that yet on earth your fame is bright,*
> *And that your names, remember'd day and night,*
> *Live on the lips of those who love you well.*

The cathedral audience was perturbed by the strange beauty of the music. As for the critics, they were unanimous in their disapproval. (One of them complained that 'when Holst begins his new *Choral Fantasia* on a six-four on G and a C sharp below that, with an air of take it or leave it, one is inclined to leave it.') This upset Vaughan Williams so much that he wrote to Holst a few days after the performance:

Dear Gustav,

I played through the fantasia again yesterday and it is *most* beautiful—I know you don't care, but I just want to tell the press that they are misbegotten abortions.

Yrs

RVW

It was not only the critics who disliked his latest works. Publishers were returning the manuscripts he sent them, and his *Twelve Songs* with words by Humbert Wolfe were refused by three firms before he found someone willing to print them. As usual, Holst remained unperturbed by the disapproval of critics or of publishers, and went on composing what he wanted to. And, as usual, he agreed to write commissioned works whenever it was possible. He even agreed to provide the music for a film called *The Bells*, which was advertised as 'adapted from the original of Sir Henry Irving's famous play'. This was in the spring of 1931. An entry in his notebook for that year says:

film 90 ft = 1 min
ft multiply by 2 divide by 3 = seconds.

His lively description of one of the studio sessions has survived in a letter to Vaughan Williams's wife:

> I have appeared in a film! At least I think I have. Or rather, I probably shall when it is developed. Unless I am 'killed in the cutting room'. They wanted more people in the crowd last Thursday so I volunteered and acted with Eric's Ma who is a dear. Eric first appeared in a film five years ago. He is now eight years old. O. B. Clarence, who is acting in the film as well as appearing in Shaw's *St. Joan* each night (and who is also a dear), told me that once they were a whole day filming a hole in the heel of his sock. Perhaps the gem in our film is when the two lovers, after a motortrip, go shopping on old London Bridge. I haven't asked why—it isn't done. But I imagine that the reason is that a replica of old London Bridge was made for the Wembley exhibition, and my film's studio is at Wembley.

The preview of *The Bells* was a painful experience. He looked white with dismay when he heard the distortion of the sound-track, and it was a great relief to him when the film was withdrawn.

Holst at work in his sound-proof music room

During the last few years of his life he had more leisure for holidays, and he enjoyed winter walks in Sicily, exploring ruined Greek temples, and April walks in Normandy, exploring ruined medieval cathedrals.

His favourite London walk was from Hammersmith bridge, past William Morris's house, along Chiswick Mall, through the narrow footpath by the church and into the gardens of Chiswick House. Most of his walks were solitary, to enable him to go on thinking of the music that was in his mind. But whenever an old friend came to London to see him he would plan a walk to celebrate the occasion.

His enjoyment of life was one of the things about him that his friends remember most clearly. One can recognize his sense of humour in his music, particularly in his last comic opera *The Wandering Scholar*, and in the 'Jazz band piece' which is now known as *Capriccio*.

He wrote the 'Jazz band piece' while he was in America. Harvard University had invited him to be Lecturer in Composition in 1932. 'I shall be free to take outside jobs, chiefly conducting,' he told a friend. 'At last, I'm learning how to conduct my own things. It's about time!'

On the voyage out he wrote home, saying: 'Owing to the vibration the only things I can read are my own scores which I have been trying to memorise while walking up and down the deck. In short, Life has been Dull. (One afternoon I began to realise why people don't like my music!)'

In New York he was able to see his brother Emil, who had been acting with the Theatre Guild. 'He is a first-rate character actor,' Holst told Vaughan Williams. 'And he has the greatest luck an artist can have: he is known and respected by everyone here who cares for real acting, and ignored by all the rest. He stayed with me and we were under one roof for the first time for forty years.' But New York, unfortunately, was full of people who wanted to interview Holst and take his photograph. 'My rest cure in N.Y. is degenerating into a business man's working day,' he complained in a letter to me. 'It is now 10 a.m. and I've been spending most of the time telephoning and making appointments. If it goes on much longer I shall hire a stenographer, a nasal voice, golf clubs and a weak liver. Unless I decide on being a star conductor. In that case I really must cultivate a more picturesque back view. How is it done?'

Life at Harvard was comparatively peaceful. He enjoyed the teaching, and his music-room was so quiet that he was able to set several of his friend Helen Waddell's translations of medieval Latin lyrics for male voices and strings or for equal voices in canon.

Canon: *Evening on the Moselle*

The last five years

His six-months' Lectureship at Harvard was interrupted by illness. 'On Easter Day', he told Vaughan Williams, 'they took me to hospital with a duodenal ulcer. And I learnt the real meaning of the phrase "A Bloody Nuisance". I had one beautiful experience. I felt I was sinking so low that I couldn't go much further and remain on earth. And, as I have always expected, it was a lovely feeling. As it began, I had a vague feeling that I ought to be thinking of my sins. But a much stronger feeling was that there was something more important on hand and that I mustn't waste time. As soon as I reached the bottom I had one clear, intense and calm feeling—that of overwhelming Gratitude. And the four chief reasons for gratitude were Music, the Cotswolds, RVW, and having known the impersonality of orchestral playing.'

He recovered from the haemorrhage, and after several weeks of convalescence he was able to hear the Harvard students give a concert of his works in his honour, which he described as the 'happiest night' he had spent in America. 'It was like Morley College on a large scale,' he wrote. 'Those youngsters sang some of my things by heart. One can't have a higher compliment than that! And the 1st trumpet of the Boston Symphony Orchestra *wanted to return his fee!!*'

When he came back to England in that summer of 1932 he was not allowed to be energetic, but he was well enough to have a holiday in the Cotswolds with his brother Emil, and they drove round Cheltenham, reminding each other of the houses they had known when they were children.

81

In spite of being ordered to live 'a restricted life' he managed to do a fair amount of work during the autumn and winter. He went on with his settings of medieval lyrics, and revelled in the intricacies of writing canons in three keys. He was able to go to concerts, and he particularly enjoyed hearing performances of new music by young composers. (After one of these concerts he met the nineteen-year-old Benjamin Britten and had five minutes conversation with him while going home on the top of a bus.)

His friends were surprised when he took up the trombone again, after nearly thirty years, in order to play in Vaughan Williams's *Fantasia on Christmas Carols* at St. Paul's Girls' School. (I can remember seeing him practising slow scales in his sound-proof room.)

He had been looking forward to helping with the Christmas music at Thaxted. But he had a relapse at the end of December, and the last year of his life was spent in and out of clinics and nursing-homes, with bouts of pain, and with only short intervals when he was able to concentrate on his music. It was during these intervals that he wrote his *Brook Green Suite* for strings, his *Lyric Movement* for viola and small orchestra, and the *Scherzo* which was to have been part of a symphony.

He was too ill to go to the first performance of *The Wandering Scholar* in January 1934. But he was able to help the St. Paul's orchestra in the first try-through of the *Brook Green Suite* in March, and he listened from his bedroom to the first broadcast performance of his *Lyric Movement*. He never heard the *Scherzo*: he just had time to finish the full score, though he found it very uncomfortable having to write it in bed.

In May he sent his greetings to the Whitsuntide singers who were having their festival at Bosham, near Chichester. 'I wish you all Good Luck,' he wrote, 'Good Weather, much playing and almost too much singing and many happy returns of the Day (I mean Days). And I wish myself the joy of your Fellowship at Whitsuntide 1935.'

He was operated on during that same week, and he died two days later, on 25th May. His ashes were buried in the north aisle of Chichester Cathedral, at the request of his friend Bishop Bell. The Whitsuntide singers came and sang *This have I done for my true love*; the dancing rhythm was a perfect comment.

XII *Centenary of his birth*

Holst used to say that composers' centenaries were a help and that 'England could do with one a week'. That was in the days when no one knew much about the English music of the sixteenth and seventeenth centuries, and if Holst happened to mention in a lecture that Dowland was as great a songwriter as Schubert, his audience would gasp with astonishment, as if he had said something quite extraordinary.

After his death, people often referred to him as a 'pioneer'. It is true that he had to struggle for many things that we now take for granted. He insisted that 'school music' should be real music. He was determined that girls should be allowed a chance to learn wind instruments. (The first woman to be admitted to the wood-wind section of the Queen's Hall Orchestra was an oboe pupil from St. Paul's Girls' School.) He proved by experience that school-children need exciting contemporary music to sing and play. (This was an unheard-of notion when he began teaching, and he must have had considerable faith to believe, while he was writing the *St. Paul's Suite*, that the day would ever come when a school orchestra would be able to play the second movement up to time.) He knew that children should be given the opportunity to listen to first-rate performances of modern works, and in the late nineteen-twenties he asked the music department of the B.B.C. if he might take some of his pupils to hear studio broadcasts of new music. (This was the origin of the 'Invitation Concerts' at the B.B.C.)

He was the first to encourage grown-up beginners to try to compose. In his amateur choirs and orchestras he refused to allow any pupils to be turned away because they were 'not good enough'. (There was a second-violinist in the Morley orchestra who had a paralysed right arm: she used to lean against the wall with her 'bowing' arm held rigid while she moved her fiddle to and fro with her other arm.)

Some of the people who heard about his amateur performances thought that he must have been an 'amateurish' sort of musician. They were wrong. With professionals his standards were ruthlessly high. I can remember walking home with him one evening when we had been listening to a disappointing recital by a young professional pianist who was a friend of his. 'You know,' he said, 'the worst of it is there is no room for the second-rate: it might just as well be the nineteenth-rate.'

Many of his beliefs are more acceptable to us today than they were to his contemporaries in the nineteen-twenties. He used to say: 'When I'm composing, I feel just like a mathematician.' This puzzled me at the time, but now I know what he meant.

During the centenary year of his birth the house where he was born was bought by his 'native town' of Cheltenham. It is now open to the public as the Holst Birthplace Museum. His piano is there, sounding very much the same as when I heard him trying out bits of *The Planets* on it in Thaxted in 1915. And there are framed manuscripts of several of the pieces he wrote when he had just left the Grammar School in Cheltenham.

Most of his manuscripts are now in the British Library. Others are in the Bodleian at Oxford and in the Parry Room Library at the Royal College of Music. A number of them are being reproduced, year by year, in the volumes of the Collected Facsimile Edition of his works.

Some of the scores that remained out of print for thirty years after his death have now been reissued, and many of his works that were seldom performed during his life have now been recorded; the list includes the once despised *Choral Fantasia* which is now recognized as one of the best things he wrote.

Among the many celebrations of his centenary, I think the most appropriate was hearing other composers saying how much they had learnt from his music. As long ago as 1917, soon after he had finished the score of *The Planets*, he wrote to one of his friends, saying: 'I believe very strongly that we are largely the result of our surroundings and that we never do anything alone. Everything that is worth doing is the result of several minds playing on each other.'

rom A Choral Fantasia

Re - joice ye dead, where - 'er your spi - rits dwell, Re - joice that

yet on earth your fame is bright, And that your names, re -

- mem - ber'd day and night, Live on the lips of those who love you well.

Gustav Holst

Dates of events in Holst's life

1874   Born 21 September in Cheltenham
1893   Went to the Royal College of Music
1898   Played trombone in the Carl Rosa Opera Company and Scottish Orchestra (until 1903)
1901   Married Isobel Harrison, 22 June
1903   Taught at James Allen's Girls' School (until 1921)
1905   Musical Director, St. Paul's Girls' School (until 1934)
1907   Musical Director, Morley College (until 1924)
1918   Private performance of *The Planets*, 29 September
       Musical Organizer for Y.M.C.A. in Near East (until 1919)
1919   Taught at University College, Reading (until 1923) and at the Royal College of Music (until 1924)
1923   Accident and concussion, February
1924   Nervous breakdown. A year's rest
1927   Holst Festival at Cheltenham, 22 March
1930   Gold medal of the Royal Philharmonic Society, 3 April
1932   Lecturer in Composition at Harvard University. Taken ill in March. Returned to England in June
1933   Continued to compose, but led the life of an invalid
1934   Died 25 May

Suggestions for further reading

Gustav Holst: a Biography, by Imogen Holst (Oxford University Press, 1938. Second edition 1969)

The Music of Gustav Holst, by Imogen Holst (Oxford University Press, 1951. Second edition 1968. Out of print; available in libraries)

Holst, by Imogen Holst (Novello Short Biographies, 1972)

Heirs and Rebels. Letters written to each other and occasional writings on music by Ralph Vaughan Williams and Gustav Holst, edited by Ursula Vaughan Williams and Imogen Holst (Oxford University Press, 1959. Reprinted Cooper Square Publishers, Inc., New York, 1974)

Gustav Holst: Letters to W. G. Whittaker, edited by Michael Short (University of Glasgow Press, 1974)

Collected Essays on Gustav Holst, by Edmund Rubbra (Triad Press, London, 1974)

A Scrap-book for the Holst Birthplace Museum, compiled by Imogen Holst (Holst Birthplace Trust, Cheltenham, 1978). This contains a facsimile of Holst's own 'List of Compositions' and many photographs

FOR REFERENCE

A Thematic Catalogue of Gustav Holst's Music, by Imogen Holst (Faber Music Ltd in association with G. & I. Holst Ltd, 1974)

Gustav Holst: A Centenary Documentation, by Michael Short (White Lion Publishers, London, 1974, now obtainable from Severn House Publishers Ltd). This includes a list of recordings and a detailed bibliography.

Select list of Holst's works

89

This have I done for my true love,
Op. 34, No. 1 (1916)
The Hymn of Jesus, Op. 37 (1917)
Ode to Death, Op. 38 (1919)
Choral Symphony, Op. 41
(1923–4)
Seven Bridges part-songs, Op. 44
(1925–6)
A Choral Fantasia, Op. 51 (1930)
Six medieval choruses, Op. 53
(1931–2)
Canons for equal voices (1932)

SOLO VOICE

Four songs for voice and violin,
Op. 35 (1916–17)
Twelve Humbert Wolfe songs,
Op. 48 (1929)

CHAMBER MUSIC

Terzetto (1925)
Six pieces for piano
(Northumbrian tunes, Nocturne
and Jig, 1924–32)

The *Collected Facsimile Edition* of the autograph manuscripts of Holst's published works is being published by Faber Music Ltd in association with G. & I. Holst Ltd, edited by Imogen Holst and Colin Matthews:

Volume I: *Chamber Operas* (Savitri, The Wandering Scholar)
Volume II: *Works for Small Orchestra* (St. Paul's Suite, A Fugal Concerto, Double Concerto, Brook Green Suite, Lyric Movement)
Volume III: The Planets
Volume IV: First Choral Symphony (in preparation)

Several early works, hitherto unpublished, are now available in Faber Music Ltd's hire library, including:

The Mystic Trumpeter, Scena for soprano and orchestra (1904, revised 1912)
Fantasia on Hampshire Folk Songs for strings (1916, revised I. Holst, 1970)
The Lure, for orchestra (1912)

In preparation:

Elegy from *The Cotswolds Symphony* (1899–1900)
Quintet in A flat for wind (1903)
Orchestral *Interlude* from Act III of *Sita* (1899–1906)
Invocation for cello and orchestra (1911)

Index

The titles of Holst's works mentioned in the text are listed together under his name. Figures in italics refer to page numbers of music examples and facsimile manuscripts.